Superhero Superstars

Benedict Cumberbatch

by Emma Huddleston

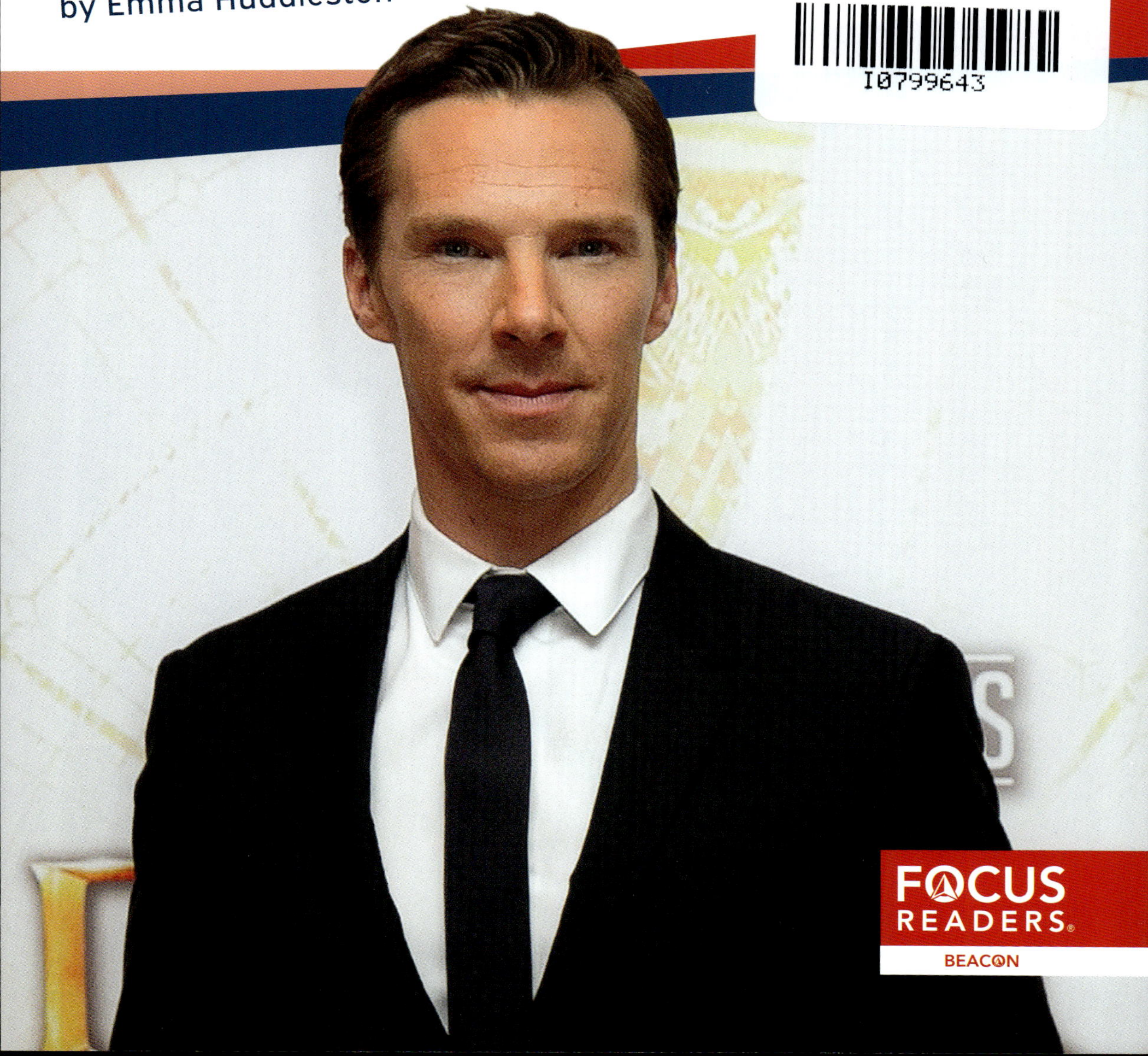

FOCUS READERS

BEACON

www.focusreaders.com

Focus Readers is distributed by North Star Editions:
sales@northstareditions.com | 888-417-0195

Produced for Focus Readers by Red Line Editorial.

Photographs ©: Joel Ryan/Invision/AP Images, cover, 1; Red Line Editorial, 4; AF archive/Marvel/Disney/Alamy, 6; Shutterstock Images, 8, 14, 17, 18, 20-21; Geraint Lewis/Alamy, 11, 12; XPX/STAR MAX/IPx/AP Images, 22, 29; LGjr-RG, PacificCoastNews/Newscom, 25; Pictorial Press Ltd/Alamy, 26

Library of Congress Cataloging-in-Publication Data
Names: Huddleston, Emma, author.
Title: Benedict Cumberbatch / Emma Huddleston.
Description: Lake Elmo, MN : Focus Readers, [2021] | Series: Superhero superstars | Includes index. | Audience: Grades 4-6
Identifiers: LCCN 2019054691 (print) | LCCN 2019054692 (ebook) | ISBN 9781644933671 (hardcover) | ISBN 9781644934432 (paperback) | ISBN 9781644935958 (pdf) | ISBN 9781644935194 (ebook)
Subjects: LCSH: Cumberbatch, Benedict, 1976---Juvenile literature. | Actors--Great Britain--Biography--Juvenile literature. | Doctor Strange (Motion picture : 2016)--Juvenile literature.
Classification: LCC PN2598.C86 H83 2021 (print) | LCC PN2598.C86 (ebook) | DDC 791.4302/8092 [B]--dc23
LC record available at https://lccn.loc.gov/2019054691
LC ebook record available at https://lccn.loc.gov/2019054692

Printed in the United States of America
Mankato, MN
082020

About the Author

Emma Huddleston lives in the Twin Cities with her husband. She enjoys writing children's books and reading mystery novels. If she could choose a superpower, it would be to read other people's minds.

Table of Contents

DOCTOR
STRANGE
MASTER OF THE MYSTIC ARTS

Chapter 1

Doctor Strange

Doctor Strange watches a **villain** approach. The villain runs forward. The villain kicks him backward. Strange crashes into a glass case with a red cape inside. The glass shatters.

People around the world read comic books about Doctor Strange, who is also known as the Sorcerer Supreme.

Doctor Strange's red cape is known as the Cloak of Levitation.

The villain swings his blade. Strange is kneeling. He has nowhere to go. Suddenly, a red cloth stops the blade. The cape seems to come alive. It saves Strange's life.

The camera stops filming. Workers move it to a new position. Meanwhile, Benedict Cumberbatch stands up. He takes a deep breath. He prepares for the next part of the scene.

The actor gets into character. He forgets his own life. He imagines the life of Doctor Strange instead.

Fun Fact

The character Doctor Strange first appeared in comic books in 1963.

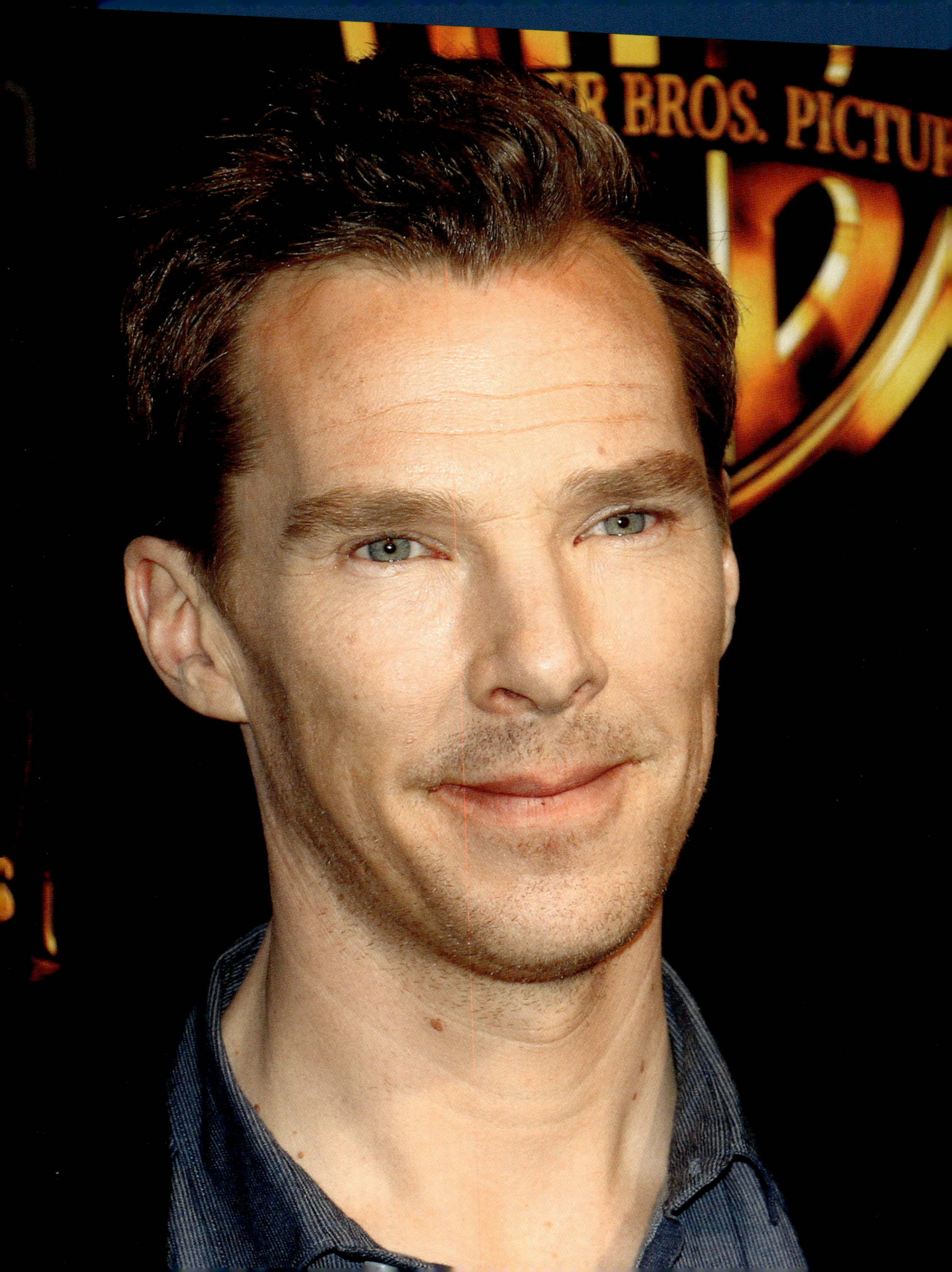

Chapter 2

Young Actor

Benedict Cumberbatch was born on July 19, 1976. He grew up in London, England. His parents are Wanda Ventham and Timothy Carlton. They are both actors, too.

Cumberbatch is a British film and theater actor.

They helped Benedict realize his love for acting at a young age.

Benedict went to school at Harrow in London. He played on the rugby team. He painted. He also started acting in his teens. He knew he wanted to be an actor when he grew up.

Fun Fact

As an adult, Cumberbatch enjoys extreme sports. For example, he enjoys skydiving, scuba diving, and snowboarding.

In addition to acting in movies, Cumberbatch also performs in plays.

Cumberbatch studied drama at Manchester University. He got a **degree** in classical acting. He also trained as an actor. He went to the London Academy of Music and Dramatic Art. He had an **agent** by the time he finished school.

In *Frankenstein*, Cumberbatch played the doctor on some nights and the monster on other nights.

Cumberbatch used his acting skills in many ways. He spoke on radio shows and starred in movies.

He acted on television and on stage. For example, he was in the play *Frankenstein*. The play had two lead **roles**. Cumberbatch played both on separate nights. He won acting awards in 2012 for the play. He has won other awards as well. Now, he is known around the world.

Fun Fact

Cumberbatch took a year off before going to university. He spent part of that year teaching English in India.

Chapter 3

Success Around the World

Cumberbatch got his big break in 2004. He played the lead role in the movie *Hawking*. Stephen Hawking was a real-life scientist. Cumberbatch also starred in a TV show. He played Sherlock Holmes.

Cumberbatch films a scene as Sherlock Holmes in 2013.

Holmes is a smart detective. The character first appeared in mystery stories in the late 1800s.

Cumberbatch is known for playing smart or gifted characters. The characters are often serious. For example, Cumberbatch played Alan Turing in one movie. Turing

Fun Fact

Cumberbatch dyed his hair black to play Sherlock Holmes. But the dye failed. It turned his hair green before filming.

Cumberbatch, acting as Alan Turing, films a scene in London in 2013.

was a math genius in real life. He helped solve difficult codes during World War II (1939–1945).

Cumberbatch was awarded a star on the Avenue of Stars in Krakow, Poland, for his acting.

Cumberbatch has also been a **voice actor**. In 2018, he was the voice of the Grinch. He was also in *Mowgli: Legend of the Jungle*. He played the tiger villain Khan.

Cumberbatch has had lots of success in his work. He wants to use his fame to help others. He also wants to bring attention to important causes. For example, Cumberbatch aids **charities**. Some of them are for children in need. Others help people with cancer.

Fun Fact

Cumberbatch played Thomas Edison in a 2017 movie. Edison was an American inventor. He helped bring about the modern age of electricity.

INSIDE HOLLYWOOD

Surprise Visit

The last day of filming for *Doctor Strange* was in New York City. That day, Cumberbatch went into a comic book store. The store was crowded. Shelves and bins of comic books filled the room. Cumberbatch was dressed in full costume. He walked around. He looked for copies of *Doctor Strange* comics. Customers were surprised to see him.

The store's owners enjoyed his visit. Cumberbatch took a picture with them. He held a *Doctor Strange* comic in his hand. The store can actually be seen in the movie. Doctor Strange runs past it.

People find many kinds of stories at a comic book store.

WOLVERINE
Fantastic Four
DOCTOR STRANGE
MASTER OF THE MYSTIC ARTS
CAPTAIN AMERICA
IRON MAN
THE INCREDIBLE HULK
THE STRANGEST MAN OF ALL TIME!!
CAPTAIN AMERICA
THE COMING OF THE FALCON!
the X-MEN
SECRET WARS
MARVEL COMICS GROUP
MARVEL TEAM-UP
SPIDER-MAN AND THE INHUMANS
THE INVINCIBLE IRON MAN
VENGEANCE! CRIES CRUSHER!
WOLVERINE
THE MAN OF STEEL
LUKE CAGE HERO FOR HIRE
Wonder Woman
Wonder Woman
BATMAN
BATMAN

Chapter 4

Special Effects

Doctor Strange has many **special effects**. They make the movie feel both real and magical. For example, the cape that saves Strange's life is only cloth. In real life, it can't move on its own.

Doctor Strange's cape gives him the ability to float and fly.

Special effects experts used computer programs to make it look like the cape was acting on its own.

Special effects changed how Cumberbatch worked. Sometimes he filmed scenes in many parts. After, experts filled in the gaps with special effects. Cumberbatch also

Fun Fact

In one scene, Doctor Strange is moving backward in time. The scene took 23 nights to film.

Experts replaced all of the green with special effects after each scene was filmed.

acted in front of green screens. These screens took the place of the actual **set**. He had to imagine where Doctor Strange was.

Doctor Strange's magical abilities are created by special effects.

Cameras filmed Cumberbatch acting as he normally would. Later, special effects experts filled in the setting. They made objects move.

They added pictures of different places. Sometimes they used many flashing images. This effect makes it look like Doctor Strange is moving through time.

Cumberbatch plays Doctor Strange in other Marvel movies. He appears in *Avengers: Infinity War* and *Avengers: Endgame*. Cumberbatch enjoys being in Marvel movies. He was excited to star in a Doctor Strange sequel.

FOCUS ON

Benedict Cumberbatch

Write your answers on a separate piece of paper.

1. Write a letter to a friend about some of the characters Benedict Cumberbatch has played.
2. If you were an actor, what types of characters would you want to play? Why?
3. When did Cumberbatch first start acting?
   A. after he graduated from school
   B. when he went to university
   C. as a teenager in high school
4. Why might acting in front of a green screen be a challenge?
   A. Actors must imagine their locations.
   B. Actors must perform their own stunts.
   C. Actors must speak directly to the camera.

5. What does **shatters** mean in this book?

Strange crashes into a glass case with a red cape inside. The glass ***shatters****.*

A. stays in one piece
B. breaks into many pieces
C. turns a different color

6. What does **genius** mean in this book?

Turing was a math ***genius*** *in real life. He helped solve difficult codes during World War II (1939–1945).*

A. a person who performs stunts in a movie
B. a person who is extremely smart or creative
C. a person who fights in a war

Answer key on page 32.

Glossary

agent
A person who helps an actor find jobs.

charities
Organizations set up to help people in need.

degree
A rank given by a college or university after someone completes a program of study.

roles
The parts actors play in a television show or movie.

set
A collection of furniture, objects, and backgrounds used for a particular scene of a movie.

special effects
Images or sounds that help make imaginary things seem real in movies or television shows.

villain
A character who works against the hero of a story.

voice actor
A person who provides the voice for a character in an animated film.

To Learn More

BOOKS

Bell, Samantha S. *You Can Work in Movies*. North Mankato, MN: Capstone Press, 2019.

Hammelef, Danielle S. *Behind-the-Scenes Movie Careers*. North Mankato, MN: Capstone Press, 2017.

McCarthy, Cecilia Pinto. *The Science of Movies*. Minneapolis: Abdo Publishing, 2017.

NOTE TO EDUCATORS

Visit **www.focusreaders.com** to find lesson plans, activities, links, and other resources related to this title.

Index

Answer Key: 1. Answers will vary; **2.** Answers will vary; **3.** C; **4.** A; **5.** B; **6.** B